MY BODY Inside and Out!

What Happens When I Grow?

by Ruth Owen

Consultant:

Suzy Gazlay, MA
Recipient, Presidential Award for Excellence in Science Teaching

Ruby Tuesday Books

Published in 2014 by Ruby Tuesday Books Ltd.

Editor: Mark J. Sachner
Designers: Tammy West and Emma Randall

Photo credits:
Science Photo Library: 7 (top), 7 (center); Shutterstock:
Cover, 1, 4–5, 6, 7 (bottom), 8–9, 11, 12, 15, 16–17,
18–19, 20, 21 (left), 23; Superstock: Cover, 13, 21 (right).

Library of Congress Control Number: 2013908619

ISBN 978-1-909673-32-8

Printed and published in the United States of America

For further information including rights and permissions
requests, please contact our Customer Service Department
at 877-337-8577.

Contents

Words shown in **bold** in the text are
explained in the glossary.

Amazing Changes

When you were born, you were less than 2 feet (60 cm) long.

You weighed just a few pounds.

You had no teeth, and your little head had just a soft fuzz of baby hair.

You couldn't walk, talk, ride a bike, or read a book.

It's amazing how much you've changed, but how did it happen? Let's check it out.

What happens when I grow?

Your Changing Skeleton

Inside your body is a framework of **bones** called a **skeleton**.

When you were born, some parts of your skeleton were made of rubbery **tissue** called **cartilage**.

As you grew from a baby to a child, the cartilage changed into hard bone.

When you were a baby, you had about 300 bones in your body.

Once you are an adult, you will have 206 bones.

That's because as you grow up, some of your baby bones join together to make bigger bones.

A model of an adult skeleton

If you want to know what cartilage feels like, touch your ear. The hard, but bendy, parts of your ear are made of cartilage.

6

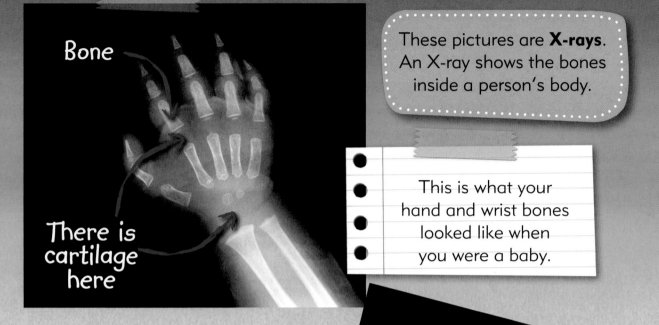

Bone

There is cartilage here

These pictures are **X-rays**. An X-ray shows the bones inside a person's body.

This is what your hand and wrist bones looked like when you were a baby.

This is what your hand and wrist looked like when you were five years old. You can see that some cartilage has turned to bone.

Bone

This is an adult's hand and wrist. All the bones have finished changing and growing.

Your Growing Bones

When you were a baby, you had tiny fingers, tiny toes, and short arms and legs.

You've grown bigger and taller because your bones have grown.

A bone grows by producing new cartilage inside itself.

Then the cartilage turns to new, hard bone.

Each time some new bone tissue grows, a bone gets a little longer.

These pictures show how a bone grows a little longer.

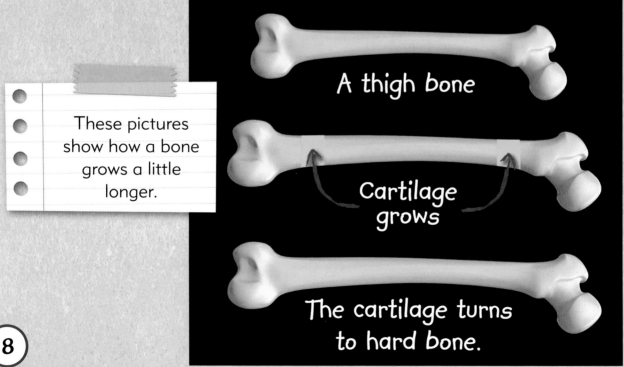

A thigh bone

Cartilage grows

The cartilage turns to hard bone.

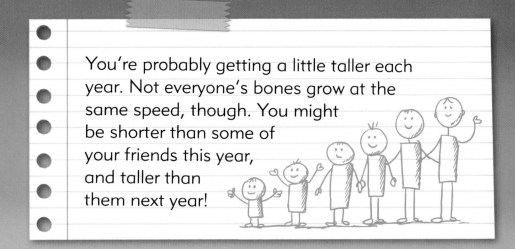

You're probably getting a little taller each year. Not everyone's bones grow at the same speed, though. You might be shorter than some of your friends this year, and taller than them next year!

As you grow, you don't just grow taller. Your hands, feet, and whole skeleton get bigger. Your bones will stop growing when you are about 25 years old.

Your bones grow wider, too. New tissue grows on the outsides of the bones to make them bigger.

Your Teeth

Your teeth started to grow during your first year.

By the time you were three or four years old, you had 20 baby teeth.

Then, when you were five or six, those teeth started to get loose and fall out.

This makes room for your **permanent** teeth that are waiting to grow from your **gums**.

By the time you are about 12, your 28 permanent teeth will have replaced your baby teeth.

Take good care of these new teeth, because they must last for your whole life!

When you are about 20, you will probably grow four more adult teeth. These teeth grow at the back of your mouth. They are called wisdom teeth. Then you will have 32 teeth in total.

A new
permanent
tooth growing

How to care for your teeth

- Brush your teeth at least two times a day.
- Use dental floss to clean bits of leftover food from between your teeth.
- Visit your dentist twice a year to get a check-up for your teeth.

When you were born, you could wave your hands and feet, but you couldn't control them.

From crawling, to walking, to running, you still had lots and lots to learn!

To understand how you've learned so much, let's start by taking a look at your amazing **brain**.

Inside your brain and the rest of your body are billions of tiny **cells** called **nerve cells**.

Your brain sends instructions to different parts of your body along pathways made of nerve cells.

Everything your body does is controlled by your brain.

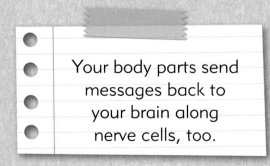

Your body parts send messages back to your brain along nerve cells, too.

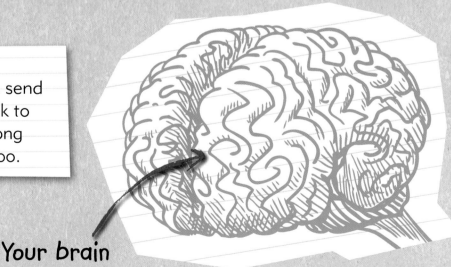

Your brain

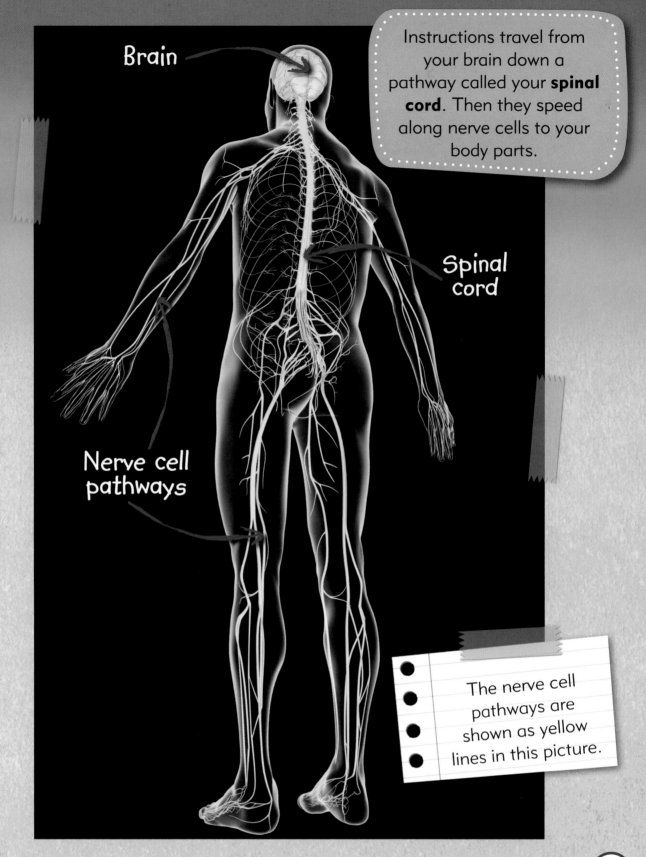

Brain

Instructions travel from your brain down a pathway called your **spinal cord**. Then they speed along nerve cells to your body parts.

Spinal cord

Nerve cell pathways

The nerve cell pathways are shown as yellow lines in this picture.

Learning to Smile

When you were born, your baby brain and body had all the nerve cells it needed.

Now your brain had to connect the nerve cells.

It had to make the pathways for instructions to travel along.

For example, when you smile, instructions go from your brain to the **muscles** in your face.

It probably took your baby brain about six weeks to make the smile pathway.

Once the pathway was made, though, you've been able to smile ever since!

During your first three years, your brain made trillions of pathways. You learned how to do more and more things.

Brain

You're on the Move

When you move your leg or arm, it's the muscles in that body part that do the moving.

Before a muscle can move, it needs instructions from your brain.

During your first year, your brain made lots of new pathways to your muscles.

Then it could send instructions along those pathways.

Soon, your brain could tell your arms and legs to crawl.

Then, the pathways were ready to tell your legs to walk!

As a baby and toddler, you had to practice all the new things you learned. That's because your muscles had to learn what your brain was telling them to do.

First
steps

You're still learning new things today. If you try a new ballet step or soccer move, you have to practice it. Then your brain and muscles learn the pathways. Soon you're spinning or kicking without thinking about it.

Ballet steps

Learning to Talk

Do you have a friend who speaks a different language than you?

It's fun to learn new words in another language.

This is exactly what you had to do when you were a baby.

You listened to people talking and copied the noises they made.

9 months old

In time, you learned that different noises, or words, meant different things.

By the time you were two or three years old, you could put words together.

Dada

Ga ga ga!

Car

I year old

Juju!

Ball

2 years old

Want juice!

Cat

You are still learning about 10 new words each day. By the time you are an adult, you will know about 100,000 different words.

When you were a baby, you could drink milk, but you couldn't eat solid food.

Now you have teeth for chewing, and your brain has made the chewing pathways.

Sometimes you probably even make your own meals.

You can talk, read, write, move around, and play sports.

It's amazing how much you've grown, changed, and learned since you were born!

Fluffy baby hair

Braided hair

You're not only much bigger than the baby you. You look very different, too!

Glossary

bone (BOHN) A hard, unbending part of your body. Bones support your muscles and other body parts.

brain (BRANE) The body part that controls your senses, thinking, and movements. Messages between your brain and other parts of your body are sent and received through nerve cells, or nerves.

cartilage (KAR-tuh-lij) Strong, rubbery tissue found in many areas of the body, including your nose and ears.

cells (SELZ) Very tiny parts of a living thing. Your bones, muscles, skin, hair, and every part of you are made of cells.

gums (GUHMZ) Soft tissue that creates a protective covering over the roots of your teeth.

muscle (MUH-suhl) A part of the body that contracts, or tightens up, and relaxes to produce movement.

nerve cell (NURV SEL) One of the billions of tiny cells that carry information between your brain and other parts of your body.

permanent (PER-muh-nint) Long lasting, never to be replaced.

skeleton (SKEL-ih-tuhn) The framework of bones that supports and protects your body.

spinal cord (SPY-nuhl KORD) A long bundle of nerve tissue that connects your brain with nearly every part of your body. Your spinal cord runs down your back and is protected by the bones of your spine.

tissue (TISH-yoo) A group of connected cells in your body that work together. Cells are very tiny parts of a living thing. Your body is made of many different types of cells including bone cells, muscle cells, and nerve cells. Muscle tissue, for example, is made up of muscle cells.

X-ray (EKS-ray) A photograph showing certain parts of the inside of your body, such as bones and teeth.

Index

Read More

DK Publishing.
First Human Body Encyclopedia (DK First Reference). New York: DK Publishing (2005).

Rowan, Kate.
I Know How My Cells Make Me Grow (Sam's Science). London: Walker (2000).

Learn More Online

To learn more about what happens when you grow, go to
www.rubytuesdaybooks.com/mybodygrow